LOVE
SAVES LIVES

SCENARIOS OF 7F

CAROL FRIERSON-CONLEE

7F Lodge

Copyright © 2021 by Carol Frierson-Conlee.

All rights reserved. No part of this book may be reproduced in any written, electronic, recording, or photocopying without written permission of the publisher or author. The exception would be in the case of brief quotations embodied in articles or reviews and pages where permission is specifically granted by the publisher or author.

7F Lodge/Love Saves Lives
www.7flodge.com
Printed in the United States of America

Although every precaution has been taken to verify the accuracy of the information contained herein, the author and publisher assume no responsibility for any errors or omissions. No liability is assumed for damages that may result from the use of information contained within.

Love Saves Lives/ Carol Frierson-Conlee -- 1st ed.

CONTENTS

Preface 1

1. Hill Country Lodge & History of 7F 3
   7F Vanilla Bread Pudding with Whiskey Sauce

2. Mexican Bungalow - Mexico 17
   Mexican Lover's Dip

3. French Chateau - France 23
   Lavender Lemon Shortbread Cookies

4. Spanish Hacienda - Spain 31
   Spanish Potato Tortilla

5. Sugar Shack - Confederacy 43
   Chicken and Sausage Gumbo

6. Batts Ferry - Texas 51
   Shrimp and Grits

7. Sully's - Texas A&M 63
   Tomato Basil Soup and Chicken Marsala

8. The Barn - USA 75
   Old Brazos Biscuit Company Cream Biscuits

9. The White Wedding Chapel 83
   White Wedding Cake Cupcakes with Cream Cheese Icing

Honoring the Journey 97

For the most magical, marvelous Craig

PREFACE

Stories, or in this case, scenarios that build on imagination, have long been a favored tool for growth and understanding, often opening "portals" that allow us to suspend our belief and somehow "become" the characters we are reading about. We can escape. We can transcend. We can engage in fantasy. Each character's emotional journey is shared intimately with us and we are immersed in their experience.

As a degreed playwright, short story writer and theatrical set designer, with a wild *unbridled* imagination and pure construction lust, I deliberately set out to create a magical, theme-styled romantic hospitality property that was built around these stories that I call scenarios. Construction started in 1996. The project of 7F was a way to preserve a sacred piece of land that I had inherited from my father, while sharing that sacred space with others.

The small tract of land was a strong morphemic field of healing for my father and his many, many Aggie Corps buddies that came to hunt there in the 1950's while trying to escape the pain and the wounds from their WWII commissioned service. It was the site of vast emotional and heartfelt recovery, and as a young child, I witnessed that healing, as they allowed their fraternal love for each other to act as their deepest balm of peace. What presented itself as a rural "deer camp" was actually a sacred chapel of light --campfire light and the inner light of their amazing love and compassion for each other. Their healing journey so long ago helped me find many solid answers to parts of my own broken life. I had to return to honor them.

This little book is a collection of poetic short story scenarios that were the foundation for each of the design concepts of the individual secluded 7F cabin suites. These scenarios are part real life, part wildly infused fictional romance and part of something elusive like a falling star. In these scenarios, restless spirits settle, sacrificed desires evaporate, the beautiful possibilities of passionate love are voiced in these pages, playing with all layers of reality, emphasizing historical and contemporary tales, each based solely on the power of the bond of love, each showing that, yes, it is so very, very true that …..LOVE SAVES LIVES.

In fact, it's the only thing that ever has.

HILL COUNTRY LODGE
&
HISTORY OF 7F

During The Depression the three Frierson brothers all attended Texas A&M College, commuting by train from the original 7F Ranch, northwest of Abilene, in Haskell County. The 7F family brand was originated there in 1886. My father was the oldest of these three brothers.

The Frierson family farmed cotton, wheat, ranched cattle and had a cattle transport trucking company that took area cattle to the rail head in Abilene and then by train into the stockyards in Ft. Worth. In 1920, when my father was just sixteen years old, he would ride on the stock train with the 7F cattle and other area ranchers' cattle and check each head of livestock into the sale pens when they arrived so that each individual lot of cattle could be registered for sale at the cattle auction there.

My grandparents, who were born in the 1800's, would then take the passenger train into downtown Ft. Worth and check into a nice hotel. My grandfather would then make the trip from town, via trolley, up to the stockyards on the north side of town. It was still called "Hell's Half Acre," due to its rough and very rugged environment. He would fetch my father from the old Wright Hotel and together they would go to the cattle sale to collect payment for the various calf crops. Then they would both return to Ft. Worth, where the family would do semi-annual shopping for 7F, dine out, buy clothing, see the sights and do some banking. A few days later, they would return together to Abilene by train, and then by car to Haskell County with all of their purchased goods following behind in transport trucks.

Each Frierson brother studied agriculture at Texas A&M College, and each was, of course, in the Corps of Cadets. Throughout their years at A&M, their only transportation to and from the campus was by train, always arriving at the old College Station Depot. The family would come to College Station once a year by train from Abilene to watch the annual year-end final review. Following their studies at A&M, each received their commission in the United States Army and after the shocking attack by the Japanese at Pearl Harbor, each brother served in WWII. Roy was in the Infantry on the French front; Byron was an artillery commander instrumental in the take over of Berlin; and my father, Gene, served in the Pacific, as an Army hospital administrator. Following the war, they returned to A&M to pursue graduate degrees and during that time, they built this first hunting cabin, which I named the Hill Country Lodge.

It appeared to be a much-needed place for healing. They gathered with their Aggie friends to hunt and, as they happily declared when organizing the gatherings, absolutely no women were ever allowed. It was a rural "man cave" as many hunting camps actually are, and certainly were back then.

Across one wall of the cabin were four sets of full-size bunk beds. In the center of the one large room was an extra-long picnic table, where food and drink and dominoes and card games stayed in circulation. There were two large refrigerators, a long kitchen area along one wall, two full-size stoves, an enormous outdoor cistern that collected rain water, an oversized outhouse, a large campfire area and a huge, loud, sputtering post-war Caterpillar diesel generator that pushed enough power through wires to illuminate the whole camp with strings of large outdoor light bulbs. It was pure heaven for these men.

When I was just six years old and in my first grade of school, that fall on the opening weekend of deer season, I was allowed to come to the deer camp with my father.

These men wanted to make an exciting spectacle of *'the very first girl ever allowed in their camp.'* This was totally a spontaneous arrangement to try and cheer up my spirits after the sudden loss of my mother, who had died the previous spring.

It was a cold, wet day in November with threats of sleet lingering from moment to moment and patches of ice were here and there all over town beneath the low grey clouds. As we were leaving the house, I jumped from the one-ton flatbed truck and ran back to my room to get a small, glass doll's bottle, in case I saw a deer. I innocently thought I might possibly catch it and feed it, and pet it. I could hardly wait as we slipped and slid down the rough, wild county roads, crossing swollen creeks, threading the big truck through pasture gates and crossing over muddy tank dams. It was the height of adventure. And it was freezing!

As is often the case with our child-like hearts, once we arrived at the camp my attentions were drawn to the numerous deer, gutted and hanging from the trees, the smell of venison sausage squealing and smoking on the grill and the smoke and heat of the blazing campfire and the laughter of the men. In this forbidden man's world, I felt like it was a right of passage I was being initiated into. Sadly, I lost the doll bottle. I must have dropped it somewhere in the camp. It was an overwhelming moment and I was totally over-stimulated.

It was much like an active, bustling scene from the TV show Mash. The men were driving old Willis army jeeps, wearing their flack-jackets that were uniforms from the war and the whole camp had the feeling of a military outpost. What throttled me most was their tender fellowship towards each other. These Aggie friends there were in need of telling each other their painful war stories with deep emotion. I remember one group of about five men that were shoring up a friend that was, yes, crying. Seeing a grown man cry with such wild abandon was frightening for me. I recall one of his wails was common for that post-war time. He kept repeating, *But why did I make it home and he didn't? Why? Tell me why?!*

You can imagine my shock, which was quickly spotted by my father and his brothers and some other close friends who stepped in to immediately distract me. I was whisked away from that part of the camp where the whiskey flowed and taken to the grill for a hamburger that was hastily made especially for me. The coke was cold and the burger was hot. The frost on my breath was billowing. I was silent and frightened for quite some time. Then, as we reversed our trip back home, I thoroughly sensed that my dad realized his good intentions to celebrate me were met with the harsh reality of PTSD and emotional residue from the war, which does not end on the battlefield; the war comes home with each one of the men that served and survived.

When I left for college in 1972 the cabin was virtually abandoned. My horse went on to greener pastures, our family matured and I stayed in the city. Daddy died in 1982 and for years I couldn't return.

Eventually funeral notices started coming to me through the telephone, and what followed were beautiful obituaries and eulogies for each of these old Ags as they passed from this mortal world and into the hereafter.

Imagine my mature mind at these funerals. I was in disbelief as I learned about their lives. One-by-one, I learned of the massive heroism each of these Aggie veterans possessed. I learned AFTER their deaths, within that same group of men, they served in every major WWII combat theater from D-Day's amphibious landing, to the take over of Berlin, the terror of the Pearl Harbor bombing, battles at Guadalcanal and Iwo Jima, the fighting along side of Rudder's Rangers, the courageous assist with Allied troops to liberate the ghastly concentration camps and those that adroitly managed mash-like field hospitals, artillery battalions and supply chains in horrific war zones across the world. I was astonished. These quiet heroes in my young life were highly decorated, all-American superheroes. I had no idea.

Throughout my friendship with each of them, not a single one ever openly shared their inner and outer battles. The war history was not discussed in front of me, and certainly not with me. Together as they gathered each hunting season at the 7F deer camp, at that original 7F Lodge, they kept each other strong, as Aggies often do. They saved each other by sharing their own grievances and heart breaks privately with one another. They truly, truly saved each other. And, eventually, they saved me, too.

After a couple of decades later, I was hiking in the Andes Mountains while studying about area anthropology in Peru when I decided to go home. I camped inside Machu Picchu one evening and crafted a 'huaca' site there for my personal meditation and prayer. It was as if I heard my father's voice guiding me to return to the cabin. So, that's what I did.

I came home to the States, then traveled straight to 7F and camped by the old cabin. The windows were broken, raccoons were living in some of the open cabinets, my mother's old Fiesta dinnerware was still in the shelves. I wept. I knew what I had to do. I had to bring that cabin back to life to honor the bond that those men held on to so tightly for their emotional survival.

Thirty-six years after the day I lost that little glass doll's bottle, I began to develop this land further, to include additional cabin themes named and designed after countries that flew a flag over Texas. While shopping for unique décor, I went to a local estate sale and met a clever and witty man that would become my husband a little over a year later and wouldn't you know it, while digging in the yard outside this little cabin, my soon-to-be husband found the little glass, rubber-nipple doll's bottle that I had lost on that day so long ago. I was completely astonished. Now this little bottle sits in a shadow box on the kitchen window there in the cabin. It was a sign, I believe, that I made the right decision to revive my father's wish, to perpetuate our family brand and to save this dear, deer hunting cabin. After all, who better in the world to find this personal artifact than the love of my life? It was such a powerful message -- truly, *a message in a bottle.*

There is an enormous amount of love in this cabin. There is a healing energy here, too. It is a most sacred site. These Aggies truly were the greatest generation. Their fine spirits are fused into so many of my beautiful memories. I feel as though they truly continue to watch over the place. And that is quite an honor.

How else could that doll's bottle have surfaced to remind me?

7F LODGE BREAD PUDDING

This is THE most requested recipe we have served at 7F.
It has been quite a tradition. For 25 years.

SIDE NOTE:
*I created this recipe to make it super-easy for our hospitality interns to prepare before our many caterings for rehearsal dinners. The students were fastidious with measuring the old recipe, which was more difficult, but we also needed to give ingredient orders to them, should they need to fetch something from town on their way to work. So, this recipe was 'rounded up' to create the extremely simple, almost laughable, list of ingredients you see below. And hey….**don't NOT try it**.*

This recipe is crazy good. Prepare to take a bow.

CREAM TOGETHER:
1 lb. butter
4 cups sugar

ADD:

12 eggs

1/4 c. good vanilla

1 quart heavy whipping cream

POUR THIS SLURRY OVER:

2 dozen hot dog buns, sliced in small pieces

ALLOW SLURRY TO SIT FOR 15 MINUTES.

Bake this at 350 degrees in a square turkey roaster pan or 2 dishes that would offer the same volume. After 30 minutes, turn the pan around and bake for another 30 minutes. The pudding should 'jiggle' a bit in the middle, but should be nice and done on the edges.

ALLOW THE FINISHED BREAD PUDDING TO SIT FOR 30 MINUTES BEFORE SERVING. IT SHOULD COLLAPSE A BIT, LIKE A SOUFFLE.

This is served best with fresh fruit and the ***whiskey sauce*** that is such a hit, some guests asked just for the whiskey sauce!

FAMOUS 7F WHISKEY SAUCE

BRING TO BOIL:
6 egg yolks
1/3 cup vanilla
3 cups heavy cream
2 cups sugar

STIR CONTINUALLY UNTIL THOROUGHLY HEATED.

ADD:
Enough corn starch slurry to thicken to reach desired consistency.

PULL FROM HEAT WHEN THICKENED.

ADD:
1/2 cup whiskey

BLEND WELL.
SERVE OVER BREAD PUDDING AND GET OUT OF THE WAY!

MEXICO CABIN SCENARIO

He saw her first from a distance. She was wearing a white cotton dress that kicked out from her ankles as she walked across the town square. At age fourteen, Pancho Villa knew by the way that she moved and by the shape of her body that she was not just any woman. She had authority. Some called it alluring, but Pancho felt it an erotic power.

When at last he was old enough to be taken seriously, he rode the seven miles by horseback to her cantina near the rocky arroyo that helped to shelter the outlaws of the unforgiving Sonoran Desert.

In this tiny tavern, Maria Flores held court every evening, listening to the tales of the banditos as they justified their looting of civilized and opulent haciendas. By their boastful stories, she could piece together a growing pattern of discontent among the countrymen of Mexico; a revolution was brewing and these justifications were merely a shallow symptom of the deep-water monster that had finally surfaced its ugly head to feed.

The night that Pancho entered the cantina she was wearing a slender red dress, leaning back against her bar, both elbows resting on the smooth, worn edge, a clear brandy snifter in her right hand, a gold bangle bracelet circumnavigating her brown wrist. In Pancho's searing eyes Maria could see a warrior not yet born.

Slowly, at first, Maria Flores quizzed the young Sonoran about his life, learning of the comings and goings of his town: the Padre that did his good works for the peasants of the area, the merchants who, by their price-gouging and crippling finance methods, held the poor consuming population in a tight grip -- slaves without the name for it -- a dutiful breed with a high sense of honor. After rounds of query, Maria knew.

Into her private chamber she took the young Pancho Villa, teaching him to have the courage and the power to lead a ragged band of men who could -- in their hands, and by their bold acts of aggression -- possibly change the fate of Mexico.

Night after night they loved and laughed, the flickering lantern chuckling with them, casting romantic shadows in their sweating faces. Their muffled voices were heard throughout the patio and beneath the colored paper lanterns. She fed him her intoxicating 'lover's dip,' washed down with specially aged tequila and fresh lime.

Finally, when the time came, at early dawn with a homemade bar of Piñon soap, Maria washed his dusty hair in her scarlet tub, filled his canteen with cool water and sent him off on his raids, her curvy silhouette framed by the heavy portal of her private doorway.

She clearly convinced him that he had a revolution to begin.

MEXICAN LOVERS DIP

IN SAUCEPAN, COMBINE:
1 cup pitted dates, each snipped into 6 pieces
1/2 cup chili sauce
1 teaspoon grated orange rind
1/2 cup orange juice
2 tablespoons grated onions
1 teaspoon red pepper chili flakes
1/2 teaspoon cayenne pepper
1 can minced hot green chilies
1 ounce unsweetened dark chocolate, grated

BRING TO A ROLLING BOIL AND REMOVE FROM THE HEAT.

STIR IN:
1/3 cup coarsely chopped toasted almonds

BLEND THOROUGHLY.

SERVE WITH SALTY TORTILLA CHIPS AND VERY SHARP CHEESE.
AND, A SPECIALLY AGED TEQUILA WITH FRESH LIME.
VIVA LA MEXICO!

FRENCH CABIN SCENARIO

On Tuesday, she methodically bundled the seven letters she'd written the week prior and tied them with a pale blue satin ribbon, each sealed with red wax, having folded the stiff parchment paper into an envelope. As promised, every day Monique Dupui cataloged and chronicled the thoughts of her idle mind, virtually journaling the clothes she chose to wear, the foods served to her by the staff, the moods of her heart and the comings and goings of her jolly footmen. Hiding by the seashore was never her forte, yet there was a sense of peace she felt in the little Provincial village. It held an unspoken charm.

It had been only two months and she was sure it had been a year. Shortly after her heart was broken by a careless lover, her father had arranged for her to flee from Paris, hiding, unknown by any, and completely free to gather her strength and her resolve for a return debut at the opening of the Opera Season.

While her father dispatched a coach full of dubious seamstresses with bolts of billowy chiffon and brocaded satins to fit Monique for ball gowns, he carefully, and with military execution, made sure the gigolo's reputation spread throughout Paris like a gas fire. Her honor was at stake.

But if it weren't for the company of her little dog, Banjo, she might not have been able to muster a laugh. Daily, as she walked on the beach, Banjo, ran with the wind, jumped at the sea gulls and barked at the foaming surf.

One afternoon she gathered her watercolors and painted Banjo's loving face by the seashore. Around the edge of a rocky point she could see another artist, a man, wrapped in a woven blanket to ward off the chill. He painted with vibrant oils pulling from his mind something not at all there before him: a tall vase of jonquil sunflowers, some reaching for the sky, some dropping their heads in surrender. In a burst of doggish joy, Banjo bolted for the man stealing his loaf of bread, knocking a clay jug of wine over in the pale, soft sand, its claret bubbling onto the small shells beneath his feet. Not easily amused, the man stood, pulling his chair back from the wreck as Monique approached with a gesture of apology.

When she gazed upon his work, she found herself speechless. In an instant, he too was unable to talk, having seen in her a beauty that he had never been able to capture, even in his tortured mind.

After an exchange of senseless words she asked his name. "Vincent," he replied. They stood shoulder to shoulder on that butter colored point, lost in the moment of the sun setting over the Mediterranean, shifting the shadows and sending sunbeams through the clouds as Banjo frolicked in the surf watching the gull's aerial combat overhead. Without words, they found their hearts joining.

In the days that followed, Monique and Vincent dined on fruits de Mer, tiny crab legs and shoreline mussels, sardines and salty anchovies, with generous portions of wine and the nutrient rich bouillabaisse the Nicoise fishermen brewed daily. She brought him lavender cookies wrapped in linen. As the hues of Vincent's paintings intensified, so did their passion: a slow, immediate burning held under control only through protocol.

But time began to close the gap. On the evening before her father was to send a coach for her return, they could honor their etiquette no longer and in a passionate instant Vincent created a turbulent moment of intimacy far, far beyond the realm of earthly pleasure and well into the celestial magnificence of creation.

Waking from the sluggish rest that followed and the comfort of the womb-like canopied bed, Monique found herself alone. An undeniable grief overcame her as she called out his name, "Vincent?" Only silence. "Vincent!"

It seemed an eternity before he stepped in from the balcony, healing her with a fast embrace. "Come see what I've painted," he whispered.

Wrapped only in a cream colored sheet, she followed him to the tiny corner near the banister. There before him on an easel, blending into the night she could see the wet canvas.

"It's called Starry, starry night," he said softly, "As I started to paint, it became evident that you have sent me far beyond the heavens and well into eternity. You have changed my life forever."

FRENCH LEMON LAVENDER SHORTBREAD COOKIES

SIFT DRY INGREDIENTS TOGETHER AND SET ASIDE:

1 cup all-purpose flour

1/2 teaspoon salt

PLACE IN MORTAR AND PESTLE:

1 tablespoon granulated sugar

1 1/2 teaspoons culinary lavender

1 teaspoon grated lemon zest

ADD TO:

1/3 cup granulated sugar

1/2 cup softened unsalted butter

CREAM TOGETHER AND ADD:

1/2 teaspoon vanilla extract

ADD:

Dry ingredients

BLEND UNTIL MIXTURE FORMS A DOUGH CHILL DOUGH FOR 30 MINUTES.

ROLLOUT TO A THICKNESS OF 1/4 INCH.
CUT INTO DESIRED SHAPES.
SPRINKLE TOPS WITH GRANULATED SUGAR.

PLACE IN FREEZER FOR 15 MINUTES

BAKE ON PARCHMENT LINED COOKIE SHEET
12-14 MINUTES
325 DEGREES

REST ON COOKIE SHEET FOR 5 MINUTES.
TRANSFER TO WIRE RACK TO COMPLETELY COOL.

WRAP IN LINEN FOR A VERY FRENCH PRESENTATION.

SPAIN CABIN SCENARIO

She saw him first at the running of the bulls in Pamplona -- not as one of the others furiously drunk on Madera and trying to prove to the watching world their bravery and stupidity, but rather at the arena, the bull-fighting ring where the enormous animals were paraded for selection and where they eventually were herded back following their slippery, twisting gallop over uneven cobblestone streets and cheering crowds.

He was in a noble position as matador near the *picador* of his childhood, carefully watching the entry of each bull into the ring as each trotted the border, slung the stringing mucus from their huge, snorting nostrils over their dense shoulders and then pausing in an oscillating discovery that there was no way out of this circle.

Each magnificent animal had a unique response to this moment, and Antonio knew how to read their minds. The picador watched with him but didn't dare gaze directly into Antonio's eyes for longer than five seconds. To hold the gaze longer during this analysis was too distracting for the serious work of observation. These animals were all speaking their great truth, and Antonio needed to know as much as possible about each bull before the fight that would take place this Sunday afternoon. Any of these animals could be the one to square off against him in the ring, and any of these could win by chance. After all, in the art of bullfighting, there is but one winner: either it is the matador or the bull. And there is death.

Esperanza had been invited and escorted to the ring by her father. It was his glorious harvest of olives and capers that had put him in such a fabulous mood. Thousands and thousands of acres of trees had once again surrendered their abundance in record tonnage, and this he had turned to gold. Ships were departing daily for ports around the world, and virtually every hold was filled with his briny crop.

Courts and palaces demanded his name be placed on every stone jar in order to insure its contents were of the finest available. Yes, this harvest was greater than ever recorded in the three hundred years of family propriety. "Magnificent," she heard him say softly. "Magnificent, Esperanza. This is the greatest of all harvests in history!"

Straining to hear his near-whisper words, she leaned forward offering a startling view of her cleavage that had been modestly covered by a lace shawl. As if carefully nudged by the universe itself, Antonio turned at the exact moment Esperanza bent forward, only to be hypnotized by her astonishing beauty and ample femininity. He turned back to the ring, but he couldn't pay attention. He returned his gaze to her, and pivoted his body in her direction. Arms by his side in straight attention, he stared straight at her, hoping for a return glance at which point her father slapped his knee and declared that it was time to go to the bodega for tapas, especially the delicious Spanish tortilla. They would return on Sunday to watch the great fight. And with that, they both rose and eased out of sight under the cover of their many servants. It was only as they descended the first of many stairs that Esperanza glanced back over her shoulder to see Antonio frozen in complete stupor. It was her shy smile and tilted chin that seared him. She turned back to descend the stairs and arrange her skirt, ever careful not to catch a heel in her ruffled hem. She smiled with amusement at the thought of that glance. Her maid had taught her early the importance of an unspoken farewell. She would see him again. She could tell by the way her legs trembled. The matador was trembling as well. He realized at that moment that he had much to live for -- much, much more to live for now.

Sunday morning came quickly for him and slowly for her. There was much to do to prepare for the bullfight. Antonio must carefully arrange for the correct foods and exercise, the right mental focus and the appropriate rituals in dressing, prayer and traveling to the arena. He was not a superstitious man, but he *was* a superstitious man. If a ritual was imperfect, then he felt imperfect, and for this reason he continued to focus only on the event at hand. Of course, he was taken by this exchange of a few days ago and it haunted him from moment to moment, but he did have a dangerous and theatrical engagement before him. The closer the time trotted to his bullfight the more he fretted. This was unusual and the constant unraveling he was fighting to ignore soon began to become too much. He had to find the priest.

Storming the cathedral on such a morning was unheard of, but exceptions had often been made for handsome matadors. He moved with a wild madness, dressed in his suit of lights and already wearing the agile footwear of a high wire performer. He moved faster, his breath heaving in and out, as his haste interrupted the prayers of others and the soft silence inside the church. At the confessional door, he moved to open it with a jerk and fell into it banging the door behind him. The attending priest recoiled with a jolt and asked, "What is it, my son?"

"What is it?" responded Antonio, "Father, you should be asking me 'Who is it?' And I should say, 'Forgive me, for I have sinned, and this time it is the worst.' It is in my mind, Father. Completely in my mind."

It would take at least a half-hour for the startled priest to hear of Antonio's fantasies about the mystery woman that had watched him for so long before he turned to see her leaving. It was in his quiet time that he was driven to impure thoughts and masculine fantasies. For as long as he had made bullfighting his career, his mind was a controllable machine, but now, he seemed incapable of any discipline whatsoever. Ritual was done correctly, but it had no meaning. Preparation was executed as always, but it was hollow. He felt like nothing mattered but to get to her, to find her, to know her and to love her in every way he knew how.

As the priest amused at yet another turning in life, he thought carefully at the odds he had placed on this fight and where it might take him financially if the matador couldn't grasp his thinking. "Tell me more about this woman," he spoke with theological adroitness. "Tell me all that you can remember and I will help you......*speak* to God." Antonio told all that he could and the Priest took careful notes. At the end of confession, the matador was given some reassurance that divine providence had a way of making all things settle out in divine order. He was dramatically blessed again by the priest, and as quickly as he departed the cathedral, so did Father Balderas. He had little time to do big work.

In the alley behind the cloister entrance, the Priest whistled for a young boy eager to help with any errand that needed speed. He was quickly dispatched with a folded envelope bearing the seal of the church and whispered instructions. The caper fields were at least a 20 minute gallop away, but the market vendors knew more through servant gossip than sentries at hacienda gates. Father Balderas accurately suspected that this woman was none other than the convent-educated daughter of Don Pedro Cuero, the most generous patron of the neighboring parish. The young boy disappeared in a cloud of dust and soon he returned after gathering the necessary information: she would be at the bullfight with her father, her mother and a great-uncle from Seville. "Gracias," the priest spoke softly as he handed the boy some coins and made the sign of the cross gently across his dirty forehead. "Thank you, my son. God will reward you."

On Sunday at the scheduled time for the bullfight, Antonio was alerted by a smiling Father Balderas as to the presence of Esperanza, her location in the prestigious seats above the entry as well as her family name, gentry and disposition. Antonio's chest swelled up with pride and determination. This fight would be for Esperanza.

Upon entering the ring and making his dramatic, overgenerous presentation to the crowd he approached Esperanza with a small bouquet of plumeria blossoms wrapped in strands of his strong, jet-black hair. The crowd roared louder as he deeply and slowly bowed before her, never knowing at that moment that in 25 passionate and powerful years together they would be seated side-by-side, above this very entry, in this very ring, hands clasped tight and hearts leaping wildly as their first son would enter the ring for his first time as matador, honoring the love of his parents' magnificent and magnetic marriage that brought him into this prestigious world of honor and fate.

SPANISH POTATO TORTILLA

Many tapas bars in Spain serve this delicious favorite.

THINLY SLICE:
 4 medium Yukon Gold potatoes, using a mandolin.

IN HEAVY SKILLET, HEAT:
1 cup olive oil

IN 3-4 MINUTES, DROP IN ONE POTATO SLICE. IF TINY BUBBLES APPEAR ON THE EDGES, THE OIL IS READY.

DROP ALL POTATO SLICES INTO THE OIL.

ADD:
1 medium onion, also sliced using a mandolin.

ALLOW POTATOES TO SOFTEN IN THIS OIL, BUT NOT CRISP.
THE POTATOES SHOULD BUBBLE LAZILY.

TEST FOR SOFTNESS, USING A SMALL KNIFE.

WHEN SOFT, DRAIN ALL CONTENTS IN A COLANDER.

BEAT:

6 large eggs
Salt & Petter

ADD POTATOES AND STIR.
ARRANGE MIXTURE IN LAYERS INTO A 10" CAST IRON SKILLET WITH 2T OLIVE OIL

COOK OVER MEDIUM HEAT UNTIL MIXTURE IS SET AND BOTTOM IS CRISP.

SLIDE OUT OF SKILLET ONTO PLATE AND CUT IN TRIANGLES.

SERVE WITH GARLIC AIOLI AND CHOPPED PARSLEY.

¡OLÉ!

SUGAR SHACK HOUSE OF BLUES CABIN SCENARIO

Ivory Joe Taylor had a love. First it was music and then it was Sadie…until Sadie left with Jasper Wallace. Jasper had come into her life on the wave of a fine man's cologne, along with his promise of better lives ahead for the both of them. Sadie with her slurry tones of sad songs and Jasper with his high style and new money, dreamed of a fast chance at fame in Memphis, at a bigger club there on the river. Known for the club's "traffic" she could be discovered in that club. Sadie only had to hear what *wasn't* said in order to pack her bags. The delta soon became history for Ivory Joe's woman-of-little-patience.

So, Sadie left with Jasper in a sputtering black automobile, leaving a trail of dust that hung in the air for days. Ivory Joe watched time go by so invisibly…as if nothing had really happened…but in truth, all he could think of was that when Sadie left all the clocks in all of the world should have stopped. She was gone -- gone for good.

She'd been gone so long that nothing but the blues would do. He cried with his guitar most every night until the sounds took on a sad, grieving tone all it's own. A local "juke joint" held open its arms and Ivory Joe held onto the friends that opened a door to that underground world of both pleasure and pain. Sure, there was his music, but somehow, in spite of the fact that life hadn't been fair at all, Ivory Joe learned that if a man did have "the gift," women would follow those notes and that music and the juke joint could become the center of a small rural universe. A rural social club in the lonely, unlit country.

So…on an offer, Ivory Joe agreed to also manage the juke joint club…*The Sugar Shack.* His songs were stiff at first, then more easy as traveling lady singers began to stroke and pet and coo. He was resistant to their cunning manipulations of his very fragile state, but soon with a reliable well-known bootlegger, some money coming in, and word of mouth bringing in patrons from as far away as across the river, Ivory Joe found his calling. He'd created an Eden…forget about needing a red apple, the "Eves" were anxious and willing to shed their skins and clothes for a chance at a "better" kind of life in a juke joint where time stood still and gin flowed and gumbo boiled.

In fact, most of the assorted women that came in and out of Ivory Joe's life were only trolling the place for a cure to their painful isolation and loneliness and that burning female need to be cultivated and sought after. Ivory Joe did little to pursue the women's desire, but by being caught up in the blues and doing a slow, steady dance with prosperity, he held an invisible magnet that pulled in their outrageous solicitations. Eventually as the nights grew long and the music died down, one by one and night after night, he would pull each of those songbirds into the serious and soulful interior of his very red room and into his very red bed.

And as their long dance of love built up the heat inside that manager's office, no matter the pleasure, the only thing Ivory Joe could think of as the lights flickered on those very red walls, was the one woman the he couldn't have. The sharp red lipstick she wore would never leave his mind. All he could ever see was Sadie. And she was gone – gone for good.

SUGAR SHACK CHICKEN AND SAUSAGE GUMBO

MAKE A 'CHOCOLATE COLORED' ROUX. MIX:
1/4 lb. real lard (!)…it's the best.
1/4 cup all purpose flour

COOK ROUX IN CAST IRON SKILLET, MELTING THE LARD ANDDING FLOUR WITH A WOODEN SPOON, STIRRING CONSTANTLY, UNTIL IT TURNS A CHOCOLATE COLOR. *DO NOT STOP STIRRING!* THIS STEP CAN TAKE UP TO 30 MINUTES.

SET ASIDE AND STIR IN THE HOLY TRINITY:
1/4 cup diced onion
1/4 cup diced celery
1/4 cup diced bell pepper

LET THIS MIXTURE SIT IN THE ROUX AND REMOVE FROM THE HEAT

IN A SEPERATE POT, BROWN:
1/2 cup Andouille sausage, diced

BROWN ON ALL SIDES, THEN ADD:]
1 cup chicken, diced

CONTINUE TO BROWN.
ADD:
1/4 cup diced onion
1/4 cup diced celery
1/4 cup diced bell pepper

ADD:
1 Tablespoon fresh minced garlic

COOK UNTIL VEGETABLES ARE SOFT.

DEGLAZE THE POT WITH:
3 cups chicken stock

WHEN STOCK COMES TO A BOIL, ADD:
Chocolate Colored Rue with Holy Trinity

WHISK CONSTANTLY TO INCORPORATE AND RETURN TO BOIL.
ADD:
1 Tablespoon Creole Seasoning
1 Bay leaf

1 Tablespoon granulated garlic

Salt to taste

ALLOW TO SIMMER FOR AN HOUR.

SERVE WITH PARBOILED WHITE RICE.
GARNISH WITH CHOPPED FRESH PARSLEY.

ENJOY WITH GREAT EUROPEAN BREAD AND A BOLD ZINFANDELL

Criminal!

BATTS FERRY CABIN

Once the waterways of the globe were the only main gateways to the discovery of new worlds. A man could "put in" on a sufficient river and connect to an ocean that connects to all the other oceans on Earth.

It cost money for passage. Shallow crossings on the muddy Brazos estuary were few and far between as the river made its way to the Gulf Coast.

Edmond Batts arrived on the East bank of the Brazos with a wagon full of rope, lumber and ambition, his team of four mules pulling the load one step at a time.

He had fallen in love in Galveston, a city filled with riches and failures and merchants wealthy from trading shiploads of timber, sugar, coffee, rum, porcelains and thick carpets to hold carved walnut furniture from the Old World.

Edmond had landed in Galveston from the distant shores of Ireland, trading his passage for an exchange of dock working and long hauling.

Through the salt grass marshes, he learned to ferry loads of cargo, poling his way through the shallows and catching the high tides and draining currents back to the channel around Galveston.

He had first seen her on The Strand in Galveston coming from a schoolhouse where she taught English to young children from around the world. The scandalous man that brought Monique here from New Orleans had drowned when a barge collided with his small skiff headed back from the Bolivar Peninsula in the dark of night. She was left alone. The man was her father and his death put her in the unenviable position of being an unprotected woman.

When Edmond arranged a chance encounter and an opportunity to walk the block with her, he could not get enough of her beauty. New Orleans held a mystery to him, but not like the others in the city. Others could not fathom a woman leaving the sophistication of the Vieux Carre for the flat sand bar of Galveston. Many thought she and her father left for a conspicuous reason since she did nothing to try and return there after his death.

She had little interest in him at first. The work she was doing with the unfortunate children was from her heart and felt it the only way she could give back to those less fortunate. She found that their scrappy ways were difficult, but for the most part the children were dear and gentle and anxious to learn. It was Edmond's tenderness with them that he displayed in honesty as he waited for her outside the school building. Over time, she began to trust him and their friendship grew. She made him her famous New Orleans shrimp and grits. They picnicked in the main park and laughed beneath the live oaks that lined its border.

Knowing that she was accustomed to the finer things, he had to take action to become a merchant in his own right. Following the finish of his servitude, he set out for the Brazos, north of Washington and he staked an area known to need safe passage. He would return for her as he made his fortune. Hopeful that she could count on him, she was challenged to believe that he would actually return for her. Losing her father left her without confidence.

As the ferry began, Edmond became known as the proprietor of Batts Ferry, the only crossing between Calvert and Washington. In no time, business was brisk. Wagons arrived before sunup, lined in a row, eager to board the ferry that was guided by rope and pulled by the mules, two mules on one side of the river and two mules on the other side of the river. One wagon would cross east and often another wagon would cross west. It became prosperous, and Edmond was becoming wealthy.

But with wealth comes another burden: no time. Passage did not wait for daylight. Often, wagons or lone riders needed to cross during the night, willing to pay the higher tariff. Edmond did not mind. His fortune was growing, but her heart was breaking.

Convinced that he had forgotten her or lost interest, anxiously she succumbed to making a visit to a "fortune teller" in the lower bowery by the dock that receives the ships from Europe. The old woman was from Hungary and was often consulted by the superstitious sailors that were sailing new routes across the sea.

Monique entered the Hungarian woman's hovel and lifted the veil from her hat. She had traveled the streets in disguise, hoping to ward off the gossip of those watching her every move.

As the fortune teller looked into Monique's eyes, she could see the heart of a woman in love. She turned over cards, she gazed into crystal balls, she burned pieces of paper and she gave her firm advice.

"The man loves you deep, but he cannot come to you. He cannot," she snapped with a thick accent.

Monique felt tears. What she heard is that he *will not* come to you, a casualty of a sad heart that is confused and crazy with love. As a tear fell from her eye, the gypsy woman continued.

"He is troubled for he cannot come. He has trouble in his heart for the longing. There is no coming for you now. Now he is not to come."

Monique wept. The gypsy pulled her chair closer to the table.

"Where is this place he will not leave? Where?"

Monique could not say. She did not know Texas.

The Hungarian snapped her fingers. "I know this man he has news on everything. You come back and he will know."

Moving to the door, the gypsy spoke again. "You can make a trip? You can travel?"

Monique was puzzled.

"You can make this trip to travel for this man that loves all of you?"

That night Monique dreamed. Edmond had a box of gold and no one to cook for him. He fell asleep on his dock and his mules were hungry. She woke with a start knowing he needed her.

The next day, again under concealed dress and via a zig-zagged path, Monique arrived at the fortune teller's door.

"Come, yes. Come. I get this man," and the gypsy sent a young boy with a message to the dock. "You like tea for now?" she offered.

With a nod, Monique took a china cup filled with thick, dark leaves and very hot water. She sipped cautiously.

"Drink all, then I read leaves for you," the woman ordered with a smile. "I love work with the lovers missing each of the other." Her accent was still thick and Slovak, but tender and motherly.

In a moment there arrived a dock worker that was a living news man. He removed his hat and took a seat after the gypsy gestured. He turned to Monique.

"There is a ferry crossing 35 miles north of Washington. It is on the Brazos River and it is where Edmond is living and working. It is the first crossing for miles and Edmond cannot leave for the work is constant. He is working himself literally to death. It is prosperous, but he is likely to die before he can come back to Galveston. He had no idea the demand in the area," the man said gently.

The reflection of the dream flooded Monique. She was close to jumping out of the room. Her anxiety was obvious.

"Drink and give me your cup. Drink." The gypsy was anxious, too.

Monique sipped and drained the liquid, handing the cup to the Hungarian who quickly turned it upside down, prayed over it and then turned it upright again. She looked carefully at the leaves.

"You must, right now, go to find him for to save him. He is calling for you, saying your name." She was emotionally invested.

Monique stood and with the assertive stance of ship captain she demanded, "Who can I pay to take me there?"

The gypsy gestured to the man who nodded.

Knowing the docks were full of charlatans and con artists, Monique had to take a quantum leap of faith. "When can we leave?"

The man mentioned he could leave in two days.

"We will leave in the morning," commanded Monique and the man nodded again.

With a handful of coins, Monique paid the gypsy and she turned to leave.

"Stop for this," said the woman as she reached in a pocket and pulled out a dried rose and some crumbled herbs. "Make this with tea when you see him first." And with the tenderness of a grandmother she handed the bundle to Monique.

It took four days of camping and long, bumpy, muddy rides in a horse-drawn wagon to get to the ferry. Rain had followed them from the coast and upon arriving at the ferry landing, Monique could see that the ferry had two buildings, one on each side of the river. With a heavy mist cloaking the water, Monique rang the bell on the East side of the ferry, barely able to see a lantern in the evening light coming from the West ferry side.

"Who needs passage? How large a load?" came a man's voice.

"Just one," Monique shouted. "It's Monique."

Edmond dove into the river and swam to her side. The ferry was not fast enough.

BATTS FERRY SHRIMP AND GRITS

IN A PAN OVER MEDIUM HEAT, MELT:

2 Tablespoons butter

ADD

1 Tablespoon fresh, minced garlic

1/4 teaspoon dried thyme leaves

1/4 teaspoon dried rosemary

1/8 teaspoon dried oregano

Black pepper to taste

SAUTE UNTIL GARLIC IS LIGHT BROWN.

DEGLAZE PAN WITH:

½ cup beer

ADD:

1/2 chicken stock

2 Tablespoons Worcestershire sauce

1 Tablespoon Creole seasoning

BRING TO HEAVY SIMMER, THEN ADD:

8 large, deveined and peeled shrimp

COOK QUICKLY UNTIL SHRIMP CURL AND SIDES TURN WHITE.

FLIP SHRIMP TO COOK BOTH SIDES. JUST ONE MINUTE.

PULL FROM HEAT AND SERVE OVER GRITS.

ALLOW LIQUID TO REDUCE AND ADD:

2 Tablespoons butter

INCORPORATE, THEN POUR SAUCE OVER SHRIMP & GRITS.

FOR GRITS:

FOLLOW PACKAGE DIRECTIONS, BUT USE MILK & BUTTER.

ADD:

1/4 Cup Romano cheese, grated

1 Tablespoon cream cheese

1/2 teaspoon salt

SULLY'S PLACE SCENARIO

Ross grew up on a small, small farm in South Texas, not far from the border, but by the standards of his parents and his grandparents, it was a good farm and in the path where the history of Texas was made.

His parents named him after a good friend that made it back from Vietnam, but died in an accident while working cattle in some old pens that gave way when a bull had had enough for the day. Ross was born a few weeks later. As he grew up, friends called him "Rock" since he'd watched, then later helped, his Dad rebuild those pens out of rock. In fact, one of Rock's first words was……..rock.

From that early age, he just knew he wanted to be a "Fightin' Texas Aggie." It was just in his blood. Oh, there were cousins that sadly preferred the other school east of A&M and Rock sat through many a Thanksgiving football massacre in front of the old black and white Zenith television at his Grandmother's frame house, just 2 miles away, but Rock never swayed from his innate desire to study at Texas A&M University. He knew he wanted to study animal science. Why not? That, too, was in his blood.

So it was, when Rock turned eighteen and pulled off that cap and gown in the football stadium after his high school graduation, he hauled hay for the summer and then loaded up his pickup with a few clothes and headed north to College Station to join the Corps of Cadets. He listened to Bob Wills on an eight track tape player mounted under the seat. Windows down, he was flying.

Coming from the other direction, in a compact car with Merle Haggard singing louder than ever, Marie sang with him, her windows down, too, thrilled at the thought of freedom from a large family and the first day of college. She had debated over attending Texas University or Texas A&M and in the end, chose that Aggie Spirit. She just knew she had to go and go she did. With a great clock radio, some new jeans, old boots and lots of hair products, she was on her way.

The big family she'd been raised in all wished her well and those still living at home lined up in the yard to wave goodbye as she backed out of the drive and past the trap where her horse leaned on the fence and gave her a look of wonder as she drove off on the county road. Her horse would not be idle long. There were five brothers and sisters ready for their chance at a 4-H ribbon. One thing a big family teaches you about is sharing.

At A&M, Rock and Marie dove into being Aggies with enormous enthusiasm. There was lots to learn and it was a great place to learn it. Instantly, they made great friends and both of them muddled through their unenviable share of mistakes. It's just that way and an unavoidable part of life. But each mistake and slight humiliation taught them more and more about life and more and more about friendship. They realized that it's the Aggie way. You can be wrong, just don't be wrong long.

Sure, they found love in those first years at school, and although it was young love, it was bittersweet. They both knew that these were the years to choose wisely and to look at life carefully. Some of their loving relationships were just not meant to be and graduate school was calling.

While friends were planning weddings and weddings were taking place, both Rock and Marie faced each day of class wearing no other ring but their Aggie ring and traveling every other weekend to watch their other Aggie friends exchange diamond rings and walk down the aisle as man and wife.

Time passed. Rock and Marie took jobs in the same department on campus, yet Rock never laid eyes on this blue-eyed country girl from Central Texas until that night at eleven o'clock, across a crowded dance floor at a popular Aggie hangout. He knew he had to meet her. She was calm, content and solid in her confidence. Unlike so many other girls eyeing the dance floor and scanning the crowd for a dance partner, she just stood there with a couple of friends, comfortable in her own skin. Refreshing.

He was intrigued. He thought, "Why is she drinking from her beer bottle out of the side of her mouth? Why had he never seen her before this moment?" He had to meet her.

This was easy, easy, easy for Rock as his parents taught him to be friendly and outgoing. He could make a connection with any stranger within moments of meeting, so Rock approached, but his pulse jumped. Whatever she wore as a fragrance enveloped him in an instant. He retreated to the bar for another look from a different point of view.

She was graceful and she seemed gentle, but not weak. She had a demeanor that he couldn't place, but it was a great comfort. She laughed and it was real. As Rock watched from a distance, a tall cowboy asked her to dance. His heart jumped, but this was a good test to see what would happen, how she could dance. Marie and the stranger moved to the dance floor.

As she danced, she floated. Her graceful movement was connected and her style was not that of a flirt, but more of a kind lady. When the dance was over, she thanked him, he tipped his hat and she returned to her friends. Rock moved in for an introduction. She turned to face him then she swallowed hard.

He had that air about him that made her comfortable. He was funny, kind and well, generous with his ear. He asked simple questions and he listened to her talk. She had a country girl's accent and a bit of a husky sound, although she was thin and fit and tan, she had a sensual lilt to what ever she said and he did all he could to keep her talking so he could hear that voice.

She agreed to a dance and then another and then at last call, they exchanged numbers. Time passed, evenings together passed, so many dances, so many turns, so many laughs, so many quarters in the juke box. So much beer!

Twelve years later, after he first made her an enticing dinner of homemade chicken marsala and tomato basil soup, she still drinks beer out of the side of her mouth for no particular reason. He can still strike up a conversation with anyone he meets, anywhere. And Rock and his blue-eyed Central Texas country girl have five little blonde haired, blue-eyed Aggies in training, some in car seats and some old enough to read the map as they make their way to family gatherings at Thanksgiving where the new generation of cousins that prefer the other school down the road take their teasing while adjusting the reception on the big, flat screen TV at Grandma's house. Some traditions are just timeless.

TOMATO BASIL SOUP

IN A LARGE SOUP POT, HEAT:
1 Tablespoon extra virgin olive oil
3 small garlic cloves, minced

COOK ABOUT 4 MINUTES UNTIL GARLIC BEGINS TO BROWN.

ADD:
4 - 14.5 cans diced fire-roasted tomatoes
1 small carton fresh cherry tomatoes, halved
2 cups chicken broth

INCREASE HEAT AND BRING TO A BOIL, THEN SIMMER.

ADD:
1 teaspoon kosher salt
1/2 teaspoon freshly ground pepper

SLOWLY POUR IN:
1 cup heavy cream

ADD:

12 fresh basil leaves, chopped

USING AN IMMERSION BLENDER OR BLENDER, PUREE THE SOUP UNTIL SMOOTH.

IF USING A STANDARD COUNTER TOP BLENDER, BLEND IN SMALL BATCHES.

WHEN SERVING, TOP WITH:

Drizzle of olive oil

Grated parmesan

THIS IS SUCH A CROWD PLEASER AND A GOLD STANDARD FOR ANY MENU.

CHICKEN MARSALA

BETWEEN SHEETS OF PLASTIC WRAP, FLATTEN:

4 boneless, skinless chicken breasts

USING A ROLLING PIN OR THE EDGE OF A PLATE, CONTINUE TO FLATTEN THE CHICKEN BREASTS UNTIL THEY ARE 1/3-1/4 INCH THICKNESS.

COAT CHICKEN WITH:

1/2 cup all purpose flour

1/2 teaspoon salt

1/4 teaspoon pepper

SHAKE OFF EXCESS FLOUR AND LET REST.
USING A 10 INCH SKILLET, HEAT:

2 Tablespoons olive oil

2 Tablespoons butter

2 cloves garlic, finely chopped

1 1/2 cups sliced fresh mushrooms

1/4 cup fresh chopped parsley

COOK FOR 5 MINUTES, STIRRING FREQUENTLY.

ADD CHICKEN TO THE SKILLET, COOKING ABOUT 8 MINUTES.
TURN THE CHICKEN ONCE AND COOK UNTIL BROWN.

TURN OFF HEAT COMPLETELY.

ADD:
1/2 cup dry Marsala wine

ALLOW THE WINE TO CREATE THE SAUCE.

SERVE WITH HOT COOKED PASTA.
GARNISH WITH FRESH PARSLEY.

BEST SERVED BY CANDLE LIGHT WITH A COLD, CRISP PINOT GRIGIO.
GIG 'EM!

THE BARN CABIN SCENARIO

Coop has spent many, many years riding everyday for the Rocking G Brand since he was barely fifteen. He left his home in DeWitt County to cowboy for the O'Connor Ranch as not as much a *runaway* as a *run ahead* kind of young man anxious to get on with his future. Rail thin with curly brown hair and shocking, almost uncomfortable, blue eyes, the older cowboys joked that he couldn't weigh one hundred and twenty-five pounds when he showed up scarred from some family pain that he was never willing to admit to. But, now he was closing in on forty and the *green hand* of decades ago was barely visible. Time and experience had made their mark.

His story of a life on the trail was told through his leathery hands, ragged face and aching joints. It was a hard life, but he was born to it. His only real home was his bedroll and his only companion was Trig, a stout Bay gelding with a smart head and alert ears. Coop had come to love Trig like a son. Their work together was an unspoken, intuitive conversation without any words. Trig just *knew* what to do and when. On Coop's look, Trig knew. On Coops rein, Trig responded. In a moment of danger, Trig stepped fast and carefully and often they worked as one.

Coop and Trig knew every creek, every bluff, and every saloon and brothel between Victoria and Kansas City. But tonight, he didn't know where he was. He had just finished the long ride taking a herd to the stockyards in KC and this would be his last. He drank more and more now, and the pain of his past with the back pain of his present never let up while he was on the trail. Whiskey was the only escape.

The trail boss, anxious to cull any weakness, told him with a sting that he'd no longer be needed. It was the whiskey that controlled his life, so he headed back to Texas alone, not sure where he'd go. Trying to fend off any emotion, he thought he might try the Cleburne Ranch. Most any good ranch needed a seasoned hand.

So, he and Trig headed south with the chill of an early winter setting in. Before nightfall, a cold and angry *northern* wind swirled and beat against his ragged neck and face. The temperature dropped across the open plains of Kansas and even the chill couldn't shake the chill in his soul. A snowfall at dusk wouldn't let up. "Blizzard!" he thought. Trig walked on.

Within hours, Trig became disoriented. A *whiteout* ensued and uncertain without perception, Trig tripped over a downed tree and panicked, sending Coop to the ground hard and unprepared. He could tell his knee was shattered. It took all of his strength to coax Trig back to him and to hoist himself into his frozen saddle. They forged on, but the cold was winning. Pneumonia soon set in, and now Coop's chills were from fever. He was delirious.

The fall dumped his last bottle of whiskey and Coop faded in and out of consciousness without any liquor. Trig knew he had to lead the way if they were to survive. Unable to follow the trail, Trig pressed on in what he felt was the right direction.

After some time, Trig approached a lone barn. Coop regained some consciousness, startled by the sound of another horse's whinny. Trig's ears perked and his pace quickened. Ahead was a cedar barn with a wide pair of doors, long runs on either side, and a hay loft above. Coop was too delirious to see the house nearby, much less get to it. Besides, Coop never asked for help. He was too proud. He made a vow at fifteen *never* to ever ask for help *again* and *never* to show any weakness.

Eleanor was considered somewhat plain by a few of the local townsfolk, but she had an inner radiance and a natural beauty still visible after years and years of hard work on this farm. It was unfortunate that she was widowed at the mere age of eighteen after a brief marriage to a young man that, above all things, made her laugh. For years she had been brokenhearted over life's misfortune and found herself often without a smile, just continuous sighing as she managed so many chores alone. She hired out labor to work her two hundred acre wheat field and split the take with the workers.

After a walloping fifteen years alone, she had long forgotten the touch of a man, a real man. In her fantasy, her husband was still alive and they were laughing and teasing each other as they watched their world grow. But in her reality, the only affection she had in her life was from her memories.

This early evening was just another cold and acrimonious night for Eleanor after another long and challenging day of tending all that was necessary to stay alive and she was ready to call it a day. Kansas offered the best in wheat fields, but the loneliest of winter nights. Months would pass with the snow blanketing everything and tonight's storm was the first of many.

Knowing that the animals still needed fresh water and perhaps some more bedding hay, she grabbed a long, green, cape-like coat, tied a black hat over her head and pulled on the thickest pair of leather gloves that she owned. She pushed through the blistering wind, fierce with snow and sleet, to get to the barn. With no visibility, she knew it was dangerous, but the job had to be done. Following the fence, she made her way to the barn.

As she opened the door to the barn, Trig snorted, and startled Eleanor. Frightened that it could be some of the last Indians in the area, she turned to find Coop on the ground burning with fever. She acted fast.

Unable to move him very far, she got him inside the barn and out of the storm. She led Trig to a stall and unsaddled him, curious by the saddlebags that held few possessions and the old, old saddle tied with a bedroll. "A cowboy headed home," she thought to herself. "He should know better than this!"

She acted fast. Maneuvering back and forth to the house, Eleanor nursed Coop for nine, long days. Finally, he woke in a haze to see her face above him and then she saw those weary blue eyes, pleading. They pierced her heart like the laughter of yesterday.

"Where am I?" he wondered. She wanted to tease him.

"You are at the Lazy 8 and you've been just that, lazy!" He buckled.

"Get me my horse and I'll be gone." He was indignant. He was hoping for whiskey and a rougher woman that knew his needs. Surely, a saloon was not that far away.

"Indians brought you in here," she teased, "and they sold you to me for about a dollar." She paused. "I bought your saddle for two and your horse for three." She waited for a response.

Coop growled at the thought.

"It was a contractual purchase: for the winter and winter only. You have nowhere to go, I suspect, and I have chores that need tending. And if you're groaning at the price, I'll have invested in feeding you and your horse for those months, so it's not the fairest trade I've ever made, but the ways of the world have brought you to my door and a deal is a deal. Fair enough?"

"I ride for a living, Ma'am. I am only on my way back to Texas to take on a new job."

She heard the word *new* and realized that he was more desperate than she'd thought. "Where?" she pushed.

"None of your business," he twisted, trying to pull himself up and out of the makeshift bed she'd made. On her look, he realized that she was looking for fun and had found a grouch. She was disappointed. Thinking she was unhappy that he'd not been grateful for the care, he backed up his sentence. "It's none of *your* business, Ma'am, because now *I* am your business." Thinking fuzzily now, he went on, "I suppose if I can get warm, by a fire, I'll be back to new and I'll start my chores just straight away." She started a small, mischievous smile.

"But if you've paid six dollars for me, my horse and my saddle, then you got taken. The last place those Indians sold me to, only paid five." They both laughed. And they kept on laughing as she helped him up and led the way to the fireplace inside the house.

By the fire that night, they ate soup and tried to tell taller tales to each other, filling the night with guffaws. At one point, Coop looked at her fresh, plain face and could see the angel that saved his life. His heart opened, which was terrifying. He needed whiskey and she knew it.

Wanting to run, he made his way up and to the door, limping, headed back to the barn and she agreed. In the months that followed, to her surprise, he would finish out the winter. But at this one moment, she expected to find him gone by sunrise. She felt sure he would run.

Hoping to prove herself wrong, she went to the barn at first light of day and to her relief, peeking in through the door, she found him sleeping. "A good sign," she thought. After returning to the house and making breakfast, she called to him with a shout that his meal was ready. Coop limped in through the door and started his first day of work with Eleanor.

Their days blended into nights with good talks and stories and always laughter. One moment, while pulling a strand of hair from her eyes, Coop was realizing that he had fallen in love with the only woman to ever really care for him. No one had ever cared for him. Ever. He was captured by her warm, caring soul, and within minutes, both their bodies found each other and entered into a night like no other. Their crazy-mad tension, finally relieved. It was an earthquake.

March third, first sign of spring and Coop was gone. He left in the night with no goodbye. Life alone and life on the trail had taught him that. But mile after mile, Coop found their passion calling him back to her barn in the woods. At one point, he stopped Trig and there they stood for an hour. So still. So silent.

Then, with firm determination, he turned Trig around and ran like the wind, back to the barn. When Eleanor came at dawn with coffee and her cream biscuits, she moved in to check on him when she noticed Trig out of breath and the saddle warm. It would be the first time he would try to out run love, but in all the countless attempts he would make in the future, he and Trig would always return, before Eleanor could ever find them gone.

Both Eleanor and Coop are buried, side-by-side, at the back edge of the outer field on a slight rise that overlooks the house and the barn. They were together until they were in their seventies, and they laughed everyday. Some days, they laughed all day long.

OLD BRAZOS BISCUIT COMPANY
CREAM BISCUITS

THESES ARE AMAZING AND WONDERFUL FOR STRAWBERRY SHORTCAKES, TOO.

GET YOUR OVEN SUPER-HOT AT 400 DEGREES.
SET OUT BUTTER AND LET IT REACH ROOM TEMPERATURE.
SET OUT JELLY, TOO.
NO COLD STUFF ON THESE HOT THINGS WHEN THEY ARE READY.
WILDFLOWER HONEY WORKS WELL, TOO.

YOU CAN THANK ME LATER. :))

OK.

IN A LARGE BOWL:
1 1/2 cups all-purpose flour
1/4 teaspoon salt
4 Tablespoons sugar (optional….but especially for shortcake biscuits)
2 teaspoons baking powder

ADD:

1 stick FROZEN butter, quickly GRATED.

CUT THE BUTTER INTO THE FLOUR

MEASURE:

3/4 cup heavy whipping cream

GENTLY INTRODUCE THE CREAM AND KNEAD THE DOUGH.
THE MORE GENTLY YOU HANDLE THE DOUGH, THE MORE TENDER THE BISCUIT.

TURN DOUGH ONTO FLOURED SURFACE AND SOFTLY PAT INTO A SQUARE.
CUT BISCUITS INTO ROUNDS…WHATEVER SIZE.

BAKE FOR 17 MINUTES ON A PARCHMENT LINED BAKING SHEET.

YOU ARE WELCOME. :)

IF YOU ALREADY HAVE COOKED THICK-CUT, SMOKED BACON TO SERVE WITH THESE BISCUITS, YOU CAN THANK ME AGAIN.

IF MAKING THESE BISCUITS FOR A BERRY SHORTCAKE, SPRINKLE TOPS WITH SUGAR BEFORE BAKING.

THE WHITE WEDDING CHAPEL

On a late afternoon in June of 1997, my then sweetheart, Craig Conlee, called me from Houston where he had been working with clients. He breathlessly said, "I should be at 7F in about an hour. Grab us something cold to drink and meet me over by the cluster of big oaks at the back edge of the property." All of this happened before cellular phone saturation, which makes the story a little more complicated. He arrived at the location before I did, which was his plan. No true roads were in place yet, as the first cabins were finishing construction and the heavy equipment needed for moving materials and trenching for plumbing, etc., would surely dismantle finished roads, so the best path for me was through the woods from the Hill Country Lodge, which was complete at that time.

I parked my truck at the cabin and walked through a trail in the yaupon to the clearing by the large trees.

There stood Craig, so proud. Around him, in a square formation, were all of the windows for a glass chapel, including the stained glass windows used in the front of the structure.

I could not wrap my head around the display and about the time I could start to manage a thought, he spoke first.

"While I was in Houston today, I went to an architectural antique dealer and found all of these beautiful windows. I think they would make the perfect wedding chapel. A white chapel."

I had discussed building a type of "novena" like I had seen all through the Yucatán and much of Central and South America -- something that held candles and offered a beautiful spiritual focal point. And?

Craig built on that idea. He went large with it. I didn't quite understand, because this was a respectable investment. He had spent some money.

As I was processing the idea, he could barely contain his excitement, which caught me a bit off-guard. It was puzzling.

Before I could speak too many words of appreciation, he turned to me and said, "Carol. Listen to me: these windows would make the PERFECT wedding chapel. A white wedding chapel. Right here. And I believe that we should be THE very first wedding ever in that little white chapel."

I was both thunderstruck and felt wildly loved. All I could really do was nod my head over and over again and hug him so hard that we both almost lost our breaths.

And, let me tell you, Craig is a salesman and entrepreneur by trade and heart, and his convincing nature can span far beyond the moment of any initial "pitch" and well into the future of wonderful possibility. He could see our future.

I'll spare you all of the smarmy details of how I said YES! and how we moved forward from there, but it's important to share that this WHITE WEDDING CHAPEL was imagined, designed and built purely from the heart. It was a real, honest-to-great-goodness, old-fashioned, romantic and fascinating wedding gift from a groom to his bride.

Honestly, can it get any better than that?

7F WHITE WEDDING CHAPEL PRAYER*

WELCOME

May you experience the presence of God in this dear little chapel and may the clear and perfect energy of Divine Love, without conditions, be with you always.

May you hear the voice of God that guides you. May you feel the joy of living that is rightfully yours. And may you come to know the freedom that comes with living a life full of gratitude.

We believe that the energy of LOVE is absolutely THE most powerful force in the Universe. We believe that God IS Love. And, we believe that when a man can stop and quieten his mind, he will hear the voice of God.

May you find these truths to serve you as they so beautifully serve us. It is our prayer for those who chance to pass this way. After all:

<u>LOVE SAVES LIVES</u>

*Written October 4, 1997; the very first wedding at 7F

WHITE WEDDING CAKE CUPCAKES or ANNIVERSARY CAKES
with Butter Cream Frosting

ARRANGE 36 CUPCAKE LINERS IN A MUFFIN TIN.
PREHEAT OVEN TO 325 DEGREES.

WHISK TOGETHER:
1 15.25 oz. box white cake mix
1 cup flour
1 cup sugar
3/4 t. salt

ADD:
1 1/3 cups water
2 Tablespoons vegetable oil
1 teaspoon almond extract
1 cup sour cream
4 egg whites

MIX WITH HAND MIXER UNTIL BLENDED.
SCOOP WITH ICE CREAM SCOOPER INTO CUPCAKE LINERS.
BAKE FOR APPROXIMATELY 18 MINUTES.
LET CUPCAKES REST FOR 30 MINUTES.

BUTTER CREAM FROSTING

CREAM TOGETHER:
3 cups powdered sugar
2 sticks room temperature, softened butter

ADD:
1 teaspoon vanilla extract
1-2 Tablespoons heavy whipping cream
Add 1 Tablespoon, at a time and blend, then add more as needed for consistency.

FILL PIPING BAG FOR DECORATIVE PIPED ICING ON CUPCAKES.

SAVOR WITH, WHAT ELSE? CHAMPAGNE!

HONORING THE JOURNEY

The start of my life at 7F was glorious and fun and full of discovery and support and delight. Then, that stopped short. Things abruptly and sadly changed for me at the age of five, when my mother's life was suddenly taken and my world took on a completely different tangent of living. The loss of my mom broke my heart and I was lost. I was thrust into what good therapists call a '1, 2, 10, 60' rapid acceleration into adulthood, but without the skills to cope with adulthood. Solid science stands strong here. It's not a natural way to evolve.

My father's wonderful old Corps buddies, those veteran Aggie hunting pals, caught me as I fell into this place of sudden abandonment and as they all watched me like hawks, they gathered together and hatched some marvelous plans to help a frightened little girl make her way through grief and fear. And? They did it in ways that men knew how to do to cope with their own major stress. Their solution? Get to work! "Let's put her to work," was their solution.

So, with the clocks off and running, a bit later, when I reached the age of eight years old, on that birthday, my father took me to his local Aggie banker where he opened up a checking account in my name that required two signatures, which included my little childish cursive handwritten name and, on the second signature line, my father's bold and dramatic autograph.

After leaving the bank that day, we soon arrived at an attorney's office where a set of documents was waiting for us in a nice, large conference room.

When the Aggie attorney arrived and greeted us, my father explained that he had arranged for a rental house to be deeded to me and placed in my name. That rental house had been purchased for me by my father. The house would be a gift. He signed some papers and the attorney's secretary brought me a coke in a bottle with a napkin wrapped around the sides. Everyone in the room was ecstatic.

In that meeting, I was also given a small monthly payment booklet for the mortgage payments for that house that were to be made to a company called The Lumberman's Investment Corporation. There in that office, using a check from my new account, I learned how to make a payment for each and every month in the amount of $76.42.

I learned how to write the check and sign the check, then how to take that check, place it in a pre-addressed envelope with the payment coupon, add the stamp and place the envelope in the mail box on the fifth day of every month. Promptly, I met the current tenant and also learned how to collect the rent and how to make a deposit into my account.

That moment was the start of me learning how to become involved in business, real estate investing and real estate management. My father, and his good friends, were showing me how to become a young business woman by teaching me some type of career I could grow into. And, those lessons were the foundation of my confident decision to build the 7F cabins as a hospitality property so many years later. I guess you could say I grew into business.

A few years after opening that first account, about the time I was entering middle school, my father and I were feeding cattle at 7F and when we were finished, I pulled up the reins on my pet horse, Smokey Joe, and as I was preparing to climb up into the saddle and ride him back to the old barn, my father paused with awe and said, "Carol, stop. Step back here into the light." The early summer sun had poked through some soft, moving clouds, and for a moment I stood in a narrow sunbeam. He slowly took the cigar from his mouth as I saw tears form in his eyes.

"When I see you in this kind of light," he said. "Right here like this, with the light coming through your hair, I can see you in the future, when you are grown. *When you are a woman.*"

I was startled as he went on. "And I want you to know that there is a great chance that you could grow up to be as beautiful as your mother." We both wept, and we awkwardly laughed with relief. I didn't know what to do but ride away with delight, hugging my horse's neck and laughing as I cried with pure joy all the way to the stalls. I knew how to run my small rental business, I just didn't know how to be someone like the mother I adored. But, he did. And he taught me that, too.

It truly was a father's blessing. A lonely daughter needs that. *Every daughter needs that.* And, of everything, EVERYTHING, he had ever taught me or had given to me in my life, this moment and those words gave me the belief that my beautiful mother lived in me and the fact that my father could see and appreciate that miracle taught me the outrageous truth that ......**LOVE SAVES LIVES.** It truly does.

In fact, it is the only thing that ever has. It sure saved mine.

BIOGRAPHY

Carol Frierson-Conlee was born 3 weeks late in a small rural Haskell County hospital during a February ice storm that arrived in the dark of night. Her first few years of life were spent on the family ranch there, moving later with her parents to Bryan-College Station so that her father could pursue additional graduate degrees from Texas A&M and eventually join the Interstate Freeway Design Team. Her mother had retired from nursing.

As a young child, in her very first letter to Santa, she asked for some boards and nails and paint so that she could build small houses where people could come and play together. She spent endless hours drawing and designing these cabin concepts using an imaginative mind and quite a few crayons.

She received a distinguished degree in playwriting from Texas Woman's University, focusing on the compelling elements of story and performance, set design and lighting.

She also received the prestigious Edith Alderman Deen scholarship for her creative writing.

As part of both a regional and national *American College Theater Festival* winning ensemble, she was proud to participate in the showcase performance at the *Kennedy Center for the Performing Arts* in Washington, DC. She toured with the once-popular *Throbbing Spatulas Comedy Troupe*, interned in experimental theaters across Texas and owned and created a highly entertaining Shakespearean dinner theater that specialized in condensed parodies of the Bard's greatest works. Even his tragedies were turned into condensed, comedic entertainment. She is currently the creative director and producer of *Little Sisters of Shakespeare.*

After 25 years of combining theatrical aspects with hospitality design by creating CHATEAU D'IVOIRE, TABOROSA, 7F LODGE and TRES LUNAS, Conlee is currently developing DOVEY'S GODDESS COLLEGE, (www.doveysgoddesscollege.com) which offers theatrically magical and musical performance art, podcasts, goddess inspired artwork, jewelry and public inspiration for women of all ages, sizes and hair colors.

She still lives a simplistic Town & Country life with her wildly supportive and entrepreneurial husband, Craig.

They live in joy and harmony and wonder and gratitude, together, sharing colorful stories, good wine and great food.

7F LODGE

7F LODGE has now been happily selling romance in the country offering secluded, individual cabin suites and destination weddings for 25 years.

Each private cabin is connected by wooded walking trails to the WHITE WEDDING CHAPEL, Bride's House and Event Center Pavilion and dance hall area near the 7F lake.

Each unique cabin is carefully designed with a casual elegance and intrinsic, yet individual charm, providing guests with a nest of indulgent comforts:

Deep, bubbling, 2 person tubs – inside and outside options
Fabulous beds with soft down pillows, comforters and upscale bedding
Spa-grade robes, towels and amenities
Very private porches `
Access to 7F on-site Wine Shop deliveries

Upscale coffee bar and condiments

Gourmet breakfast basket and pastry box with famous *Brazos Muffins*

Microwave and minibar refrigerator

Selected music that fits each cabin theme and atmosphere

And, here is the best part:

7F offers true peace and a deeply intimate escape from the outside world.

So close.

And yet so, SO far away.

www.7flodge.com

979.690.0073